Dying to Be
BEAUTIFUL

The Real Facts About Potentially
<u>Harmful</u> Cosmetic Ingredients

PETER LAMAS

Strength
& Honor

BRONZE
BOW PUB.

The information in this book is for educational purposes only and is not recommended as a means of diagnosing or treating an illness. Neither the publisher nor author is engaged in rendering professional advice or services to the individual reader. All matters regarding physical and mental health should be supervised by a health practitioner knowledgeable in treating that particular condition. Neither the author nor the publisher shall be liable or responsible for any loss, injury, or damage allegedly arising from any information or suggestion in this book.

Dying to Be Beautiful
Copyright © 2003 Peter Lamas
All Scripture quotations, unless otherwise indicated, are taken from the Holy Bible, New International Version®. NIV®. Copyright © 1973, 1978, 1984 by International Bible Society. Used by permission of Zondervan Publishing House. All rights reserved.
ISBN 1-932458-04-2
Published by Bronze Bow Publishing, Inc.,
2600 East 26th Street, Minneapolis, MN 55406.
You can reach us on the Internet at
WWW.BRONZEBOWPUBLISHING.COM
Literary development and cover/interior design by
Koechel Peterson & Associates, Inc., Minneapolis, Minnesota.
Manufactured in the United States of America

CONTENTS

BOOKS BY PETER LAMAS

Beauty & Health Glossary
Beauty Basics
Dying to Be Beautiful
The Truth About Sun Exposure
Ultimate Anti-Aging Secrets

ABOUT THE AUTHOR

 PETER LAMAS is Founder and Chairman of Lamas Beauty International, one of the fastest growing and respected natural beauty products manufacturers in the United States. He has been a major force in the beauty industry for more than 30 years. Peter's career began in New York City as an apprentice to trailblazers Vidal Sassoon and Paul Mitchell, providing the opportunity to work with some of the most famous and beautiful women of our time. His expertise in the areas of hair care, skin care, and makeup has given him a client list that reads like a *who's who of celebrities*.

His work has spanned numerous films, television, video, and print projects, including designing the gorgeous makeup used on the set of the epic film, *Titanic*. Peter has worked with the great names in fashion and beauty photography, including Richard Avedon, Irving Penn, and Francesco Scavullo. His work has been seen in photo shoots in leading magazines, such as *Vogue, Harper's Bazaar, Glamour, and Mademoiselle*.

Peter regularly appears on television and in the media in North and South America, Europe, and Asia. He travels extensively across the globe, speaking to women of many different cultures about how they can realize their potential to be beautiful both inside and out, especially educating them about the facts and myths on beauty products.

Cuban born Peter Lamas immigrated to New

York in 1961. Several years later, while pursuing a career as a commercial artist, Peter decided to finance his education by doing hair and makeup. As a result, he discovered he not only had a flair for doing hair and makeup, but he truly enjoyed helping each client look her best.

Peter's life has been dedicated to helping women feel good about themselves, by helping them realize their vast potential for personal beauty. To him, beauty is not just about the perfect haircut or makeup; it's about the full package. He can make just about any woman look absolutely stunning; but if she doesn't feel beautiful, she won't be. Beauty is very personal, and contrary to the cliché "that beauty is in the eye of the beholder," he came to realize that it is also in the eye of the possessor, because what makes us truly attractive to others is the projection of our self-esteem. Grace, confidence, and personality play a major role in attractiveness.

Peter's web site, www.lamasbeauty.com, is one of the largest women's beauty and health information resources on the Internet, through which he and a host of contributing writers keep women and men informed on important beauty and health topics.

Mr. Lamas is an innovative product developer in the cosmetics industry and recently received the distinguished honor from Health Magazine for developing the "Best Moisturizer of the Year." You can learn more about Peter's company, Lamas Beauty International, by visiting www.lamasbeauty.com or emailing him directly at peterlamas@lamasbeauty.com.

CHAPTER ONE

The Deadly CULPRIT

"My people are destroyed
from lack of knowledge." HOSEA 4:6

OVER the last 30 years of working in the
"world of beauty," I have had the
immeasurable pleasure of helping thousands of
women and men discover the secrets to beautifying
themselves—both outwardly and inwardly. I love to
see the transformation that comes in a person's life
when they begin to feel good about themselves
because they are confident in their looks. I count it a
fantastic privilege to work so closely with people
through cosmetics and make a difference in their lives.

But as is true of all good things, there is a dark
side to the beauty industry. It is not an overstatement

to say in an age when people are driven to follow a celebrity culture that people are *Dying to Be Beautiful*. I have seen far too many tragedies related to the extreme pursuit of outward beauty—from life-threatening eating disorders to quick-fix diets to fortunes being wasted on spurious beauty treatments to workout regimes that end up with repetitive stress injuries. I have seen the damage of herbal supplements sold as weight-loss pills, such as fen-phen. I believe that high-protein diets will take their toll on the liver, heart, and kidneys. I am concerned about the long-term effects for those who take hGH (Human Growth Hormone) and DHEA supplements. Most of us are aware of these through the attention that the media has raised on these issues.

What amazes me, though, is that there is almost no attention given to the fact that there are potentially harmful ingredients that are widespread throughout the cosmetic and beauty industry. When I read through books on nurturing beautiful skin, I find the focus on all sorts of outward and inward enemies of healthy skin, but I seldom read anything about examining the contents of the beauty-care products that are being applied directly on the skin.

Everyday most of us use a whole array of hair, skin, body, and beauty products without ever asking the question of whether they are safe or not. If we do take the time to read through the list of ingredients in tiny print, we have no idea whether they are good for us. Most of us assume that the Food and Drug Administration (FDA) has such tight regulations on these products that we need not concern ourselves . . . and I have discovered that is definitively not the case.

DID YOU KNOW?

It did not take me long in the business to learn that almost all cosmetics can cause allergic reactions in certain individuals. I often saw the first signs of a reaction to a cosmetic product—the burning sensation, the irritation, the mild redness, or pimples and rashes. I found out that nearly one-quarter of the people questioned in a 1994 FDA cosmetics survey responded "yes" to having suffered an allergic reaction to personal care products, including moisturizers, foundations, and eye shadows. But rather than report these products to the FDA, most people simply stop using the products. And then there are the thousands of people who are presently suffering from adverse effects and reactions from cosmetic products, and they don't realize the source of the problem.

What I didn't realize was that while many chemicals used in cosmetics never cause visible signs of toxicity on the skin, they do contain potent systemic toxins that can remain in the body for a very long time. And when you consider that some of these products get applied day after day for decades, the potential for problems is very real.

Another fact I've learned is that terms such as "natural" and "hypoallergenic" on skin-care products may be nothing more than slick advertising. When the FDA tried to establish official definitions for the use of certain terms, its regulations were overturned in court. Most of the terms have considerable market value in promoting what you think are "safe" cosmetic products, but dermatologists say they have very little medical meaning. Let the buyer beware because there is no industry-wide standard.

For years the cosmetic manufacturers suggested that the absorption of chemicals through the skin was so minimal that no worry should be given to it. Over the past few years, the emergence of the patch as an efficient way to get medication into the bloodstream shows how efficiently the skin works in delivering chemicals to the whole body . . . and how wrong the manufacturers were. Many commonly used products contain potentially harmful ingredients that are

constituted by very small molecules that easily penetrate the skin, enter the bloodstream, and build up in
the liver, kidneys, heart, lungs, and tissues—similar
to if you eat them in contaminated food. Your skin is
a major organ for absorbing substances into your
bloodstream.

While I am not a scientist or a medical researcher,
I have gathered the information in this book over the
years in relationship to advice I give my clients. It is
simply the basics of what I've learned. And here is
one example of a major problem I have found in the
industry.

WHAT SCIENCE SAYS ABOUT
SODIUM LAURYL SULFATE

Most health-conscious consumers are aware of
sodium lauryl sulfate, the most common ingredient
found in shampoos, and its potential health dangers.
But just how dangerous is this synthetic foaming
agent and cleansing detergent? A study cited in the
Wall Street Journal linked sodium lauryl sulfate to
cataracts and nitrate absorption (nitrates are cancer-
causing substances), while a major dermatology pub-
lication suggested the chemical induced contact dermatitis. In its final report on the safety of sodium

lauryl sulfate, the Journal of the American College of Toxicology stated that it has a "degenerative effect on the cell membranes because of its protein denaturing properties." The journal also added, "High levels of skin penetration may occur at even low use concentration."

Here, some additional notes from the Journal on sodium lauryl sulfate:

- Carcinogenic nitrosamines can form in the manufacturing of sodium lauryl sulfate or by its interaction with other nitrogen-bearing ingredients within a formulation using this ingredient.
- Other studies have indicated that sodium lauryl sulfate enters and maintains residual levels in the heart, liver, lungs, and brain from skin contact. This poses the question of whether it could be a serious potential health threat from its use in shampoos, cleansers, and toothpastes.
- Additional studies have found that sodium lauryl sulfate is heavily deposited on the skin surface and in the hair follicles. Damage to the hair follicle could result from such deposition.

Used mainly because it is inexpensive and produces that rich lather we all associate with cleanliness, sodium lauryl sulfate usually composes about 50 percent of most shampoos that list it as an ingredient;

about 40 percent of the product is water, and the remaining 10 percent comprises preservatives, fragrance, and color. And what about those natural extracts? They're often included in the water content (in other words, the herbal ingredients are watered down) and make up less than 1 percent of the total product. There are alternate ingredients that may be used to achieve that rich lather. They are much safer but are more expensive to produce, and therefore they are not used by most beauty manufacturers. None of my Lamas Beauty products contain sodium lauryl sulfate.

Given such suggestive evidence, and the fact that sodium lauryl sulfate is still used in most personal care products, it is a far wiser choice to simply steer clear of products that contain this chemical, especially with regard to children. In the past few years it has been easier than ever to take a healthier alternative route, thanks to pioneering research that has given birth to a new generation of natural hair-care ingredients for the health-driven consumer.

As difficult as it may sound, the only safe way to avoid unsafe beauty products is to read labels and learn the chemical jargon. In Chapter Three, I list the chemicals that I believe may be hazardous to your health, but it is by no means exhaustive. In fairness, the reader should understand there are experts who have alternative evaluations of these chemicals and do not believe they are dangerous. I believe, and many experts believe, it is the long-term effects of these chemicals that we must become aware of if we want to avoid the potential risks to our health . . . and the health of the ones we love. We never need to be dying to be beautiful.

CHAPTER TWO

Big Business and YOUR SKIN

WHEN you think about the cosmetic industry in North America, consider that it has over $30 billion in sales every year. Shampoo sales alone are over $2 billion. And before a drop of shampoo ever touches a human head, millions of dollars in development, packaging, and advertising costs have already been spent. Glossy television campaigns promise thick, strong, and healthy hair so full of shine you almost need sunglasses to get through the commercial. But behind the shimmering image they're selling you is a real product, and as a consumer you are left to evaluate whether to believe the claims or not.

In such an intensely competitive market, it would be extremely naïve to believe that the cosmetic companies put your health before their profit margins. They won't be quick to tell you that over 90 percent of all the ingredients in commercially available cosmetic products are of synthetic origin, and that many of those ingredients may be associated with health risks. Or that over 90 percent of the chemicals used in fragrances are synthetic compounds derived from petroleum. Or that all these products penetrate the skin.

Think the threat isn't real? From 1978 to 1980, the FDA analyzed 300 cosmetic samples for carcinogenic contamination. Forty percent of the samples analyzed contained carcinogens. Things actually got worse the next time they analyzed cosmetic samples. In 1991–92, they found that 65 percent of the cosmetic products sampled contained carcinogenic contaminants.

So before you buy into all the hype about how a "new and approved" product will transform your sagging, wrinkled skin to youthful vibrancy, ask yourself what might be in it. In an article published in a 1998 *U.S. News and World Report*, it was estimated that we are exposed to over 200 synthetic chemicals every day (not that we're aware of it), and some of them are delivering potential irritants, carcinogens, toxins, and hormone disrupters to our bodies.

If your health antenna is up, surely you have to wonder when a toothpaste or soap label has the warning, "Keep out of reach of children under 6 years of age." What's in that product that necessitates the warning? Or when you see that some mouthwash contains even higher alcohol concentrations than beer, wine, and liquor, you have wonder what it's doing to you. Mouthwashes that contain more than 25 percent alcohol can be dangerous to young children—one ounce can cause seizures and brain damage and five ounces can kill! According to the National Cancer Institute, mouthwash with over 25 percent alcohol concentration increases the risk of oral and throat cancer by 60 percent for men and 90 percent for women compared to those who do not use mouthwash.

WHY THE SKIN IS SO VULNERABLE

The skin, perhaps more than any other aspect of our body, effectively reflects our life and experience. Yet it is also the most vulnerable. Skin is the largest organ of our body. Stretching out from 16 to 20 square feet, it accounts for about 15 percent of our body weight. By its exposure it is continually threatened by the ravages of time and the unpredictable effects of the environment. Safeguarding its health and appearance, at every age, is extremely important for all of us, women and men alike.

The psychological effects of changes in our appearance, and especially the aging process, determine our state of mind as powerfully as physical changes are reflected in the body. Our looks are a fundamental part of our sense of self. And, at best, they provide us with a sense of confidence and well-being in our personal and social relations. Thanks to today's scientific advances in technology and what research has learned about the functioning of skin, the ability to take care of one's skin and maintain its fitness has become possible for everyone, not just the privileged, wealthy few.

Our skin is a wonderful, living, breathing organ that never stops changing, growing—or needing your attention and help to be beautiful. It forms a waterproof protective barrier against invasion by outside organisms and protects underlying tissues and organs from abrasion and other injury. It helps keep vital elements such as moisture and heat in, and its pigments shield the body from the dangerous ultraviolet rays in sunlight. The skin's fat cells act as insulation against cold; and when the body overheats, the skin's extensive small blood vessels carry warm blood near the surface where it is cooled. And because of our skin's countless nerve endings, it is responsible for our sense of touch, which allows us to sense pain, pleasure, heat, and pressure.

THE FIVE MOST IMPORTANT FUNCTIONS OF SKIN

- **Elimination:** All day, every day, skin removes toxins and debris as it sheds dead cells.
- **Secretion**: Skin's many sebaceous and sweat glands help the body eliminate oil and perspiration.
- **Reproduction:** New cells are constantly being born through cell division in the basal skin layer. In young skin, on average, the process takes 28 days. But as we age, cell reproduction slows down. By 70 or 80, new cells can take up to 37 days to develop.
- **Respiration:** Your skin can't live without oxygen. It's crucial to cell life and renewal. The skin gets its oxygen supply two ways: from oxygen-bearing blood circulating through the cells and by drawing it in from the air.
- **Moisture Control:** It's key to healthy, young-looking skin. Healthy skin maintains its moisture balance

naturally. Moisturizers assist by adding even more moisture to the skin and locking it onto the surface. Firmness, suppleness, and smoothness are determined by your skin's moisture content.

I have already mentioned that the skin absorbs whatever it is put in contact with, similar to a sponge. And yet there are hundreds of ingredients used in personal care products that are suspected or proven to be cancer-causing agents, carcinogens, irritants, dioxins, toxins, and hormone disrupters. Whether it is harmful chemicals in a household cleaner or in a cream lotion, they will find their way into our blood.

Now for a look at the list.

CHAPTER THREE

Potentially Harmful
CHEMICALS

For centuries men and women have gone to surprising lengths in their pursuit of beauty. In her legendary quest to be the most beautiful Queen of the Nile, Cleopatra's beauty products were also thought to be poisonous. She was willing to do whatever it took to be dazzling. The European cosmetic known as *ceruse* was used faithfully—and fatally, because it was mainly white lead—by wealthy women from the second century until well into the nineteenth century to make their faces look fashionably pale.

We may be doing the same today, although perhaps not to that extreme, and not be aware of it. A number of cosmetic products are made up of ingredients that could be harmful to your health. Since the FDA has not set standards for the safety testing of cosmetics, it's up to you to be your own watchdog.

I recognize that professional opinions vary widely on the safety of most of the following chemicals. Many will say that given their low levels of concentration in cosmetic products that they are perfectly safe, and the research may substantiate that to date. I can't argue against that position. My concern is that little long-term research has been done, and that it is the cumulative effect of these low levels of contaminants added to all the other daily environmental pollutants that build up in our bodies to harm our health. If there are safer alternatives in other cosmetic products, we're foolish to not use them.

Acetamide MEA: Used to retain moisture in cream blusher and lipsticks. It can cause adverse reactions and is considered toxic and carcinogenic.

Acetone: Used as a strong solvent to remove fingernail polish. It is on the EPA hazardous waste list. It can act as a depressant to the central nervous system through inhalation, resulting in dryness of the mouth and throat, dizziness, nausea, slurred speech, and drowsiness.

Alcohol: Used as an antifoaming agent as well as a water and oil solvent. It dries quickly, and if synthetically produced can cause adverse reactions.

Alkyl-phenol-ethoxylades: Used in shampoo. It can cause adverse reactions and is considered toxic and carcinogenic. Has been found to reduce male sperm count and to mimic estrogen in the body.

Alpha-Hydroxy Acids or AHAs: Used in moisturizers, toners, cleansers, masks, and age-spot removers. AHAs are known for accelerating the exfoliation of dead skin cells. But they can also increase the skin's sensitivity to the sun by as much as 50 percent, leaving you exposed to accelerated skin aging and the possibility of skin cancer. AHA delivers a smooth finish by stripping the outer layer of the epidermis and cutting into the protective barrier, causing the irritated skin to puff up and thus fill in the lines and wrinkles. AHAs are best used at a concentration that is less than 10 percent. The FDA warns that strengths over 3 percent may thin the skin.

Aluminum: Used as a color additive in cosmetics, especially eye shadow. Another form of aluminum is used in deodorants and antiperspirants, which get applied close to the body's upper lymph glandular system. It stops pores from functioning properly in the areas it is applied. Listed as carcinogenic and toxic, and when concentrated it can lead to cell mutations, which links it to cancer.

Ammonium Laureth Sulfate: Used in hair and bubble bath products. It contains ether and is easily absorbed by the skin. It can cause adverse reactions and is considered toxic and carcinogenic.

Bentonite: Used in facial mask, makeup, and face powder. A porous clay that expands many times its dry volume as it absorbs water, it may clog pores and suffocate the skin.

Benzaldehyde: Used in perfume and cologne and many other products. It can act as a depressant to the central nervous system through inhalation, resulting in dryness of the mouth and throat, eyes, skin, lungs and GI tract, causing nausea and abdominal pain.

Benzene: Used in combination with other chemicals in many personal care products. It can cause adverse reactions and is considered toxic and carcinogenic.

Benzyl Acetate: Used in perfume and cologne and many other products. It is considered carcinogenic with links to pancreatic cancer. Vapors irritate the eyes and respiratory passages.

Benzyl Alcohol: Used in perfume and cologne and many other products. It can act as a depressant to the central nervous system through inhalation, resulting in dryness of the mouth and throat, irritation to the upper respiratory tract, dizziness, nausea, slurred speech, and drowsiness.

Bronopol or 2-bromo-2-nitropropane-1,3-diol: Used in cosmetics and many leading brands of baby products. Acts by releasing nitrites, which combine with DEA to form nitrosamines.

Butylated Hydroxianisole (BHA) and/or Butylated Hydroxytoluene: Used in cosmetics and personal care products as preservatives. BHA is an animal carcinogen, suspected human carcinogen, and a xenoestrogen. BHA should not be confused with beta-hydroxy acid (salicylic acid), which is an exfoliant.

Camphor: Used in perfume and cologne and many other products. It dilates blood vessels and produces a cooling effect on the skin, but can cause skin irritation and dermatitis with repeated use. Inhalation can cause an irritation of the eyes, nose, and throat. Ingestion can lead to a burning sensation in the throat and chest, nausea, vomiting, diarrhea, headache, confusion, convulsions, and unconsciousness.

Carbomer 934, 940, 941, 960, 961 C: Used as a thickener and stabilizer in creams, toothpaste, eye makeup, and bath products. It is a known allergen that has a high acidic pH in 1 percent water solution.

Coal Tar: Used in shampoos and hair dyes. Also under the names FD, FDC, or FD&C color. Coal tar is known to be carcinogenic and causes potentially severe allergic reactions, asthma attacks, fatigue, nervousness, headaches, nausea, lack of concentration, and cancer.

Cocamide DEA: Used in shampoos and derived from coconut fatty acids. Nitrosamines can form in all cosmetic ingredients containing amines and amino derivatives with nitrogen compounds. When DEA is applied to skin, known carcinogens can form.

Crystalline Silica: Used in some personal care products and toiletries. A carcinogen with possible links to lung cancer.

DEA (diethanolamine): Also referred to as TEA. A synthetic solvent, detergent, and humectant used in liquid soaps, shampoos, conditioners, and many other products. Irritates skin, eyes, mucous membranes. Health risk especially to infants and young children. Forms nitrosamines known to be carcinogens. Causes allergic reactions and contact dermatitis. Hazardous and toxic. Stay away from these products.

Dibutyl Phthalate: Used in fingernail polish. Suspected to be linked with a high rate of fertility problems in young women.

Dimethylamine: Secondary amines cause allergic dermatitis and have carcinogenic properties.

Dioform: Used in toothpastes and other tooth

whiteners. Damages your teeth enamel by weakening their protective shell.

Dioxins: Recently added to the list of known carcinogens.

Elastin: Supposed to improve the elasticity of the skin when applied externally; however, there is no proof. It is a protein in connective tissue.

Ethanol: Used in perfumes, hair spray, shampoo, and many other products. It is on the EPA hazardous waste list. It can act as a depressant to the central nervous system through inhalation, resulting in dryness of the mouth and throat, dizziness, nausea, slurred speech, and drowsiness.

Ethyl acetate: Used as a solvent in nail polish and nail-polish remover. It is on the EPA hazardous waste list and an irritant to the eyes and respiratory tract. May cause headache and narcosis (stupor) and have a defatting effect on skin and may cause drying and cracking.

FDC-n (FD&C): Pigments that come in a variety of colors. Some are simply irritants while others are strong carcinogens. Most are coal-tar derived, and many scientists feel that adequate safety levels have not been established for each color category.

Fluoride: *Merck's Index*, the main reference of the pharmaceutical profession, lists the industrial uses of fluoride compounds as "an insecticide, particularly for ants and roaches." Under the heading "Human Toxicity," the Index says, "Severe symptoms result from ingestion of 0.25 to 0.45 grams and death results from ingestion of 4 grams." The FDA requires a warning on all fluoride toothpaste: "If more than used for brushing is accidentally swallowed, get medical help or contact a Poison Control Center right away."

Fluorocarbons: A colorless, nonflammable gas or liquid commonly used as a propellant in hair spray. Can produce mild upper respiratory tract irritation.

Formaldehyde: Used in nail polish and hardeners, shampoos, soaps, and skin creams. This potentially irritating disinfectant, germicide, fungicide, and preservative can be absorbed into the skin and cause allergic reactions, inflammation, headaches, even asthma. It is often referred to as formalin or DMDM hydantoin or MDM hydantoin. It is very toxic when inhaled and a suspected carcinogen that is linked to cancer. Its use in cosmetics is banned in Japan and Sweden. Read labels carefully. Products containing levels that might trigger an adverse reaction are required to carry a caution.

Glycols (group): Used as a humectant (emulsifier/moisturizer). In most cases it is used as a cheap glycerine substitute. Propylene glycol has caused liver abnormalities and kidney damage in laboratory animals. Diethylene glycol and carbitol are considered toxic. Ethylene glycol is a suspected bladder carcinogen. The FDA cautions manufacturers that glycols may cause adverse reactions in users.

Hydantoin DMDM: Used in the synthesis of lubricants and resins and is derived from methanol. It causes dermatitis, acts as a preservative, may release formaldehyde, and is a suspected carcinogen.

Imidazolidinyl Urea: After parabens, this is the second most commonly used preservative in many cosmetic products. It causes dermatitis and is a formaldehyde-releasing preservative.

Isopropyl Alcohol: Used in hair color rinses, body rubs, hand lotions, aftershave, fragrances, and many other cosmetics. This is a petroleum-derived solvent and denaturant (poisonous substance that changes another substance's natural qualities). Inhalation or ingestion of the vapor may cause the poisoning symptoms of headaches, flushing, dizziness, mental depression, nausea, vomiting, and coma. Has been implicated in mouth, tongue, and throat cancers with mouthwashes having an alcohol content of 25 percent or more.

Kaolin: Used in cosmetic foundations as well as powders and blushers. It is a natural clay mineral (silicate of aluminum) that may smother and weaken the skin.

Lauramide DEA: Used as a base for soaps, detergents, and laurel alcohol because of their foaming properties. It is a lauric acid derived mostly from coconut oil and laurel oil. Nitrosamines can form in all cosmetic ingredients containing amines and amino derivatives with nitrogen compounds, and nitrosamines are known carcinogens.

Limonene: Used in perfume and cologne and many other products. An irritant to the skin and eyes that is considered carcinogenic.

Linalool: Used in perfume and cologne and many other products. It can cause central nervous system disorder.

Lye or Sodium Hydroxide or Potassium Hydroxide: Combined with animal fats to make bar soaps and also found in some toothpastes and other products. It is a highly concentrated watery solution of sodium hydroxide or potassium hydroxide. It is corrosive and can be poisonous.

Methyl Chloroisothiazolinine or Kathon CG: Causes adverse reactions and is toxic and carcinogenic.

Methylene Chloride: Used in perfume and cologne and many other products. Banned by the FDA in 1988, but no enforcement is possible due to trade secret laws protecting the chemical fragrance industry. It is carcinogenic and can cause central nervous system disorder.

Methyl Methacrylate: Used in nail products, primarily used in application of acrylic nails. The chemical has been linked to fungal infections, nail deformities, and other problems. Prolonged exposure can lead to eye, skin, and lung irritation, abnormal liver or kidney function, nervous system damage, or reproductive problems. Stick with salons that use ethyl methacrylate, a safer bonding liquid, instead.

Mineral Oil: Used in makeup removers, lipsticks, and lotions. It is a petroleum derivative (crude oil) and has been linked to everything from clogged pores to acne and other disorders. Its density does not allow the skin to breathe and absorb moisture and nutrition or to release toxins. Mineral oils are listed as known carcinogens in the National Toxicology Program. It may be that it is the contaminant hydrocarbons that are the carcinogens, not the mineral oil itself. Most experts advise to avoid it.

PABA or Para-Aminobenzoic Acid: Used in sunscreen lotions. It is water-soluble vitamin found in B complex that can cause photosensitivity and contact dermatitis and allergic eczema.

Parabens: Trademark for butyl, ethyl, germa,

methyl, and propyl paraben. It is the most common preservative used in a variety of personal care products, especially creams and lotions. Petroleum based.

Para-phenylenediamine or PPD: Used extensively in permanent and dark hair dyes. It is carcinogenic when oxidized and is linked to a variety of cancers, including non-Hodgkin's lymphoma and multiple myeloma. Jackie Kennedy Onassis used it to dye her hair dark brown every four weeks or so and died of non-Hodgkin's lymphoma.

PEG (200-400): Abbreviation for polyethylene glycol, polyoxethylene, polygocol, and polyether glycol. Contributes to stripping the natural moisture and nutrition from the skin, leaving the immune system vulnerable. Many allergic reactions as well as hives and eczema are known to occur from these synthetic plant glycols.

Petrolatum: A petroleum-based product that works much the same as mineral oil to smother the skin.

Phthalates: Used in cosmetic and personal care products, especially nail polish, perfumes, hair sprays, and skin lotions. Phthalates are regulated as toxic substances under environmental laws that limit their discharge into the air, land, and water, but there are no limitations on the amount of phthalates used in consumer products, including cosmetics. Health effects of a large exposure to phthalates include damage to the liver and kidneys, birth defects, decreased sperm counts, testicular cancer, early puberty onset in girls, early breast development in girls and boys, and other reproductive disorders. While phthalate levels in cosmetics are low, there is a growing concern about the cumulative effect of this toxic substance.

Phenoxyethanol: Used as a common cosmetic preservative. Can cause severe allergic reactions. Trade names—Arosol, Dowanol EPH, Phenyl Cellosolve, Phenoxethol, Phenoxetol, and Phenonip.

Phosphoric Acid: Used as a pH adjuster in cosmetic and skin-care products. As an inorganic phosphate acid it is very disruptive to the skin if used in high concentrations.

α-Pinene: Used in perfume and cologne and many other products. It is a sensitizer that can damage the immune system.

Polysorbate-n (20-85): Used as an emulsifier in cosmetic creams, lotions, cream deodorants, baby oil, and suntan lotions. Can cause contact sensitivity and irritation to skin.

Propylene Glycol or PG: Used in suntan lotions, lipsticks, shampoos, and conditioners. It is a petrochemical solvent used as a humectant to retain moisture content when applied to the skin and viscosity to the product being used. It is the most common moisture carrying vehicle other than water that is used. But it has also been linked to liver abnormalities and kidney damage. It is also known as an irritant to the skin and eyes and nasal and respiratory passages. Avoid it altogether and instead opt for alternative products containing glycerin or sorbitol.

Sodium Cyanide: Causes adverse reactions and is considered carcinogenic and toxic.

Sodium Fluoride: Has been shown to be a potential carcinogen.

Sodium Laureth Sulfate: Used mainly in shampoo and conditioners. It is a close relative to sodium lauryl sulfate that causes skin irritation and dermatitis. Has ether added and is toxic.

Sodium Lauryl Sulfate or SLS: Used in bubble baths, toothpastes, shampoos, conditioners, and lotions. This detergent, which has been found to enter the brain, heart, and liver and impair the immune system, has been linked to eye irritations, skin rashes, and allergic reactions. The biggest problems occur when it is mixed with other chemicals, like those typically used in toiletries, because it can form carcinogenic compounds. Minimize the risks by using products with SLS sparingly and rinsing off quickly afterward.

Sodium Oleth Sulfate: May contain dangerous levels of ethylene oxide and/or dioxane, both potent toxins.

Sodium PCA (NAPCA): Used in skin and hair conditioners. The synthetic version can seriously dry the skin and cause allergic reactions. There is a plant-derived version of Sodium PCA that does not cause these reactions.

Stearamidopropyl Tetrasodium EDTA: Nitrosamines can form in all cosmetic ingredients containing amines and amino derivatives with nitrogen compounds. Nitrosamines are known carcinogens.

Styrene Monomer: Can cause adverse reactions and is considered carcinogenic and toxic. May be irritating to the eyes and mucous membranes.

Talc: Used in makeup and body powders. It is derived in powder form from the mineral magnesium silicate. Mineral talc has been linked to ovarian cancer. Another irritant in talc is mica, which can cause respiratory problems if inhaled. Avoid using talc-based powders, especially on genital areas.

g-Terpinene: Used in perfume and cologne and many other products. Can cause asthma and central nervous system disorders.

a-Terpineol: Used as a fragrance in perfume and cologne and many other products. Highly irritating to mucous membranes and can cause central nervous system and respiratory depression and headaches.

Toluene: Used as a solvent in cosmetics, especially nail polish and dyes. Obtained from petroleum, it resembles benzene, and if ingested may cause mild anemia, liver damage, irritate the skin and respiratory tract.

Triethanolamine (TEA): Used as pH balancer. Can cause severe facial dermatitis, irritation, and sensitivity. Reacts with stearic acid to form oil in water emulsions, typically lotions. May contain nitrosamines, known carcinogens.

CHAPTER FOUR

Hair Color PRODUCTS

Looking in the mirror, who hasn't found a reason to be dissatisfied with their hair color at one time or another? Lifelessly dull hair or the onset of gray cry out for the glorious shimmer and renewal of years promised by a good hair coloring. Here today, gone tomorrow, is right at your fingertips. But the warning labels on the packages, the fact that gloves are required, and the harsh chemical scents make you think twice. However, the only way to get your hair to where you'd like it to be is the chemical treatment way.

Why is that? Because it requires the chemical solution to cause the hair to swell and then the dyes can penetrate the hair cuticle to some extent and deposit its color. If that dye does not adhere to the hair shaft, as is the case with temporary hair colors, they must be reapplied after every shampooing.

IS IT HARMFUL?

As noted before, people can be allergic to a wide range of potentially harmful ingredients in beauty products. But hair color products are considered by many healthcare experts to pose the most serious emergency level problems. There are several potentially harmful ingredients to link the reactions to, depending on the type of color—permanent, semi-permanent, demi-permanent—that is being applied.

Karen M. Shelton, founder of HairBoutique.com and lamasbeauty.com contributor, says, "Almost all coloring products that lighten hair contain some amount of hydrogen peroxide. This colorless liquid achieves two major actions. It will first break down the natural melanin in the hair shaft, which instantly 'lifts' the color of the hair making it lighter. The peroxide also releases oxygen, which combines with the dye molecules and helps them to develop and deposit color. The depositing part is important for covering gray. Although many people worry about the toxicity of using hydrogen peroxide on their hair, there are more potentially toxic ingredients."

Permanent hair colors—oxidation and progressive types—are the most popular hair dye products. Oxidation hair dye products consist of a solution of dye intermediates, such as para-phenylenediamine (PPD), which form hair dyes on chemical reaction, and preformed dyes, such as 2-nitro-para-phenylenediamine, which already are dyes and are added to achieve the intended shades in an aqueous, ammoniacal vehicle containing soap, detergents, and conditioning agents. Another oxidation hair dye uses a solution of hydrogen peroxide in water or a cream lotion. Some experts think that the number of allergic reactions to hair coloring is related to PPD, while others point to ammonia, peroxide, or diaminobenzene.

Potential allergic reactions to PPD include facial and neck swelling and, if swallowed, vomiting. If PPD is inhaled directly, it may be toxic and cause coughing, sneezing, shortness of breath, and, in some rare cases, cyanosis (blue lips). In extreme cases respiratory distress has been reported and medical attention should be sought immediately. Shelton adds that when PPD makes contact with the skin, it may cause rashes and contact dermatitis. Eye contact may cause irritation, redness, and pain. Corneal damage and loss of vision has been reported in rare cases. Chronic exposures to PPD may affect kidney or liver function.

Progressive hair dye products contain lead acetate as the active ingredient. Lead acetate is approved as a color additive for coloring hair on the scalp at prescribed concentrations. Progressive hair dyes react with the sulfur of hair keratin and oxidize the hair surface to change the color of hair gradually from light colors to almost black, if desired.

Semi-permanent hair coloring products are solutions of various coal-tar, i.e. synthetic organic, dyes which deposit and adhere to the hair shaft to a greater or lesser extent. Shelton says that aniline dyes are liquid chemicals derived from coal tar and used in commercial semi-permanent hair dyes. The various aniline dyes are often considered to be toxic and irritating to the eyes, skin, and mucous membranes. Hypersensitive people may experience allergic reactions to these dyes. Historically, these dyes have also been proven to cause blindness in some cases when used in the eye areas.

Only permanent hair dye has been linked to cancer. Semi-permanent or wash-out dyes have not been associated with the disease. A U.S. study published in

2001 found that regular use of permanent color could increase the risk of bladder cancer by up to three times if the dye was used monthly for more than 15 years. It has been suggested that people with a certain genetic profile may excrete the hair dye chemicals from the body more slowly than others, giving them longer exposure to damaging substances. Another study found that using black or dark brown dye for more than 10 years was associated with a small increase in the risk of death from non-Hodgkin's lymphoma. However, some argue that it's hard to tell whether these results are merely coincidental. Two large studies in the U.S., one involving more than 570,000 women and the other involving 120,000, found no link between the use of hair dye and any adverse effect. Researchers from the National Cancer Institute estimate 20 percent of all cases among women of non-Hodgkin's lymphoma, the disease that killed Jacqueline Kennedy Onassis (who dyed her hair for four decades), are due to women's use of commercial hair dye products. Further studies have shown that due to the industry's chemical environment, hair-care professionals have a four times higher risk rate of contracting multiple myeloma (a form of bone cancer) than does the general population.

Ammoniated mercury and related metallic chemicals also provide bleaching agents that encourage color lift. Like PPD and other hair color chemicals, allergic reactions have also been linked to these particular chemicals which may or may not appear in current hair color formulations.

If you know after reading the labels that you might be allergic to some of the chemicals in hair coloring products, take preventive measures. Everyone who is going to color their hair should perform a patch test before every hair color application. No matter how many times you have used the product successfully in the past, it is impossible to predict what ingredients may cause allergic reactions or when problems may develop.

How do you know what chemicals are in your hair color brands? Read the labels or ask your colorist to tell you.

"ALL NATURAL" AND "NON-TOXIC" HAIR COLORS

There are mild coloring products on the market, such as those from Herbavita, that are safer because they have lower chemical bases. That may mean a significantly lower PPD or hydrogen peroxide level and possibly no ammonia, but one still needs to look through the list of ingredients to see what is there.

However, Shelton states that a coloring product that is as natural and mild as possible won't have the lightening and coloring power of a standard product. For instance, the Herbatint line from Herbavita is a semi-permanent coloring product that will lift color 1 to 2 levels, cover gray, and deposit pigment, but it will not help a dark haired brunette become a platinum blonde. The lower levels of PPD and peroxide make it impossible for the product to produce more dramatic results.

While the cancer risks associated with semi-permanent hair dye remain unproven, no one can say there is no health risk. The risk does not compare to the risk one takes when they smoke, but it is a risk that needs to be considered. If you choose to dye your hair at home, make certain that you follow the instructions on the packet. These usually include wearing gloves, carrying out a patch test, and watching for any possible reaction.

CHAPTER FIVE

Why Are There So Few Government REGULATIONS?

T HE regulatory requirements governing the sale of cosmetics are not as stringent as those that apply to other products regulated by the Food and Drug Administration (FDA). The FDA is only able to regulate cosmetics after products are released to the marketplace. Neither cosmetic products nor cosmetic ingredients are reviewed or approved by the FDA before they are sold to the public. This means that manufacturers may use any ingredient or raw material, except for color additives and a few prohibited substances, to market a product without a government review or approval. The FDA cannot require companies to do safety testing of their cosmetic products before marketing. The FDA does not have the authority to require manufacturers to register their cosmetic establishments, file data on ingredients, or report cosmetic-related injuries. To keep abreast of such information, the FDA maintains a voluntary data collection program. Cosmetic companies that wish to participate in the program forward data to the FDA.

If, however, the safety of a cosmetic product has not been substantiated, the product's label must read: "WARNING: The safety of this product has not been determined." In addition, the Fair Packaging and Labeling Act requires an ingredient declaration on every cosmetic product offered for sale to consumers. These regulations require that ingredients be listed in descending order of quantity. Water, for example, accounts for the bulk of most skin-care products, which is why it usually appears first on these products.

"Consumers believe that 'if it's on the market, it can't hurt me,' " says John E. Bailey, Ph.D., director of the FDA's Office of Colors and Cosmetics. "And this belief is sometimes wrong."

The FDA's challenge comes in proving that a product is harmful under conditions of use or that it is improperly labeled. Only then can the agency take action to remove adulterated or misbranded products from the marketplace.

Many ingredients were given special exemption from bans when the Food, Drug, and Cosmetic Act was passed in 1938. The FDA can't order them removed from the market even if proven harmful. Over 884 ingredients were "grandfathered in" for use in personal care products and many are suspected or proven to be cancer-causing agents, carcinogens, toxins, dioxins, irritants, and contaminants found commonly in personal care products. Companies selling personal care products can also hide controversial or dangerous ingredients under the label of "trade secrets." Because of intense competition in the industry, if a company believes it uses an ingredient that is relatively new to the industry, or that it makes their product unique, it can petition the FDA (in Canada the HPB—Health Protection Branch) to prevent disclosure of that ingredient by granting trade secret status.

IS IT A COSMETIC OR A DRUG OR BOTH?

The FD&C Act defines cosmetics as articles intended to be applied to the human body for cleansing, beautifying, promoting attractiveness, or altering the appearance without affecting the body's structure or functions. This definition includes skin-care creams, lotions, powders and sprays, perfumes, lipsticks, fingernail polishes, eye and facial makeup, permanent waves, hair colors, deodorants, baby products, bath oils, bubble baths, and mouth-washes, as well as any material intended for use as a component of a cosmetic product.

Products that intend to treat or prevent disease or otherwise affect structure or function of the human body are considered drugs. Cosmetics that make therapeutic claims are regulated as drugs and cosmetics and must meet the labeling requirements for both. A good way to tell if you're buying a cosmetic that is also regulated as a drug is to see if the first ingredient listed is an "active ingredient." The active ingredient is the chemical that makes the product effective, and the manufacturer must have proof that it's safe for its intended use. For products that are both drugs and cosmetics, the regulations require that active ingredients be listed first on these products, followed by the list of cosmetic ingredients in order of decreasing predominance.

Before products with both a cosmetic and drug classification can be marketed, they must be scientif-ically proven safe and effective for their therapeutic claims. If they are not, FDA considers them to be misbranded and can take regulatory action.

NO GUARANTEES

According to a study of cosmetic reactions conducted by the North American Contact Dermatitis Group, preservatives are the second most common cause of allergic and irritant reactions to cosmetics. Fragrances are number one. People who have had allergic reactions to cosmetics may try hypoallergenic or allergy-tested products. These are, however, only a partial solution for some and no solution at all for others.

"Hypoallergenic can mean almost anything to anybody," says John Bailey. "Hypo" means "less than," and hypoallergenic means only that the manufacturer feels that the product is less likely than others to cause an allergic reaction. Although some manufacturers do clinical testing, others may simply omit perfumes or other common problem-causing ingredients. But there are no regulatory standards on what constitutes hypoallergenic. Likewise, label claims that a product is "dermatologist-tested," "sensitivity tested," "allergy tested," or "nonirritating" carry no guarantee that it won't cause reactions.

Like hypoallergenic, "natural" can mean anything to anybody. "There are no standards for what natural means," says Bailey. "They could wave a tube [of plant extract] over the bottle and declare it natural. Who's to say what they're actually using?" Even when natural plant extracts are used, the base formulas are probably the same as other conventional products. And a natural extract does not mean it cannot cause an allergic reaction, such as Vitamin E, which is a potent sensitizer. Natural doesn't mean pure or clean or perfect either. According to the cosmetic trade journal *Drug and Cosmetic Industry*, "All plants [including those used in cosmetics] can be heavily contaminated with bacteria, and pesticides and chemical fertilizers are widely used to improve crop yields."

SO WHAT ARE YOU BUYING?

The ingredient list on a cosmetic container is the only place where a consumer can readily find out the truth about what he or she is buying. Consumers can check the listing to identify substances they wish to avoid. And becoming familiar with what cosmetics contain can help counter some of the alluring appeal showcased elsewhere on the product.

Consumers can obtain specific information about a cosmetic ingredient in various references, such as the *International Cosmetic Ingredient Dictionary and Handbook* published by the Cosmetic, Toiletry, and Fragrance Association (www.ctfa.org), available at most public libraries or at the Office of the Federal Register, 1100 L St., N.W., Washington, DC 20408. The FDA recognizes the association as a reliable source of substances that have been identified as cosmetic ingredients, as well as their definitions and trade names.

SAFETY TIPS FROM THE FDA

Besides never putting on makeup while driving, which can lead to scratching your eyeball and causing bacteria to contaminate the cut, consumers should follow other precautions to protect themselves and the quality of their cosmetics:

1. Keep makeup containers tightly closed except when in use.
2. Keep makeup out of the sunlight. Light and heat can degrade preservatives.
3. Don't use eye cosmetics if you have an eye infection, such as conjunctivitis, and throw away all

products you were using when you first discovered the infection.

4. Never add any liquid to bring the product back to its original consistency. Adding water or, even worse, saliva could introduce bacteria that could easily grow out of control.

5. Never share.

6. Throw makeup away if the color changes or an odor develops. Preservatives can degrade over time and may no longer be able to fight bacteria.

Except for color additives and a few prohibited ingredients, a cosmetic manufacturer may use any ingredient or raw material and market the final product without government approval. The prohibited ingredients are:

1. biothionol
2. hexachlorophene
3. mercury compounds (except under certain conditions as preservatives in eye cosmetics)
4. vinyl chloride and zirconium salts in aerosol products
5. halogenated salicylanilides
6. chloroform
7. methylene chloride

Consumers should report cosmetic adverse reactions by calling their local FDA office, listed in the Blue Pages of the telephone book, or the FDA's Office of Consumer Affairs at 1-800-532-4440. More information on cosmetics is available by calling the Office of Cosmetics and Colors' automated information line at 1-800-270-8869.

CHAPTER SIX

A Word About
COSMETIC
SURGERY

THE purpose of this book was to deal with the potentially harmful chemicals that are widespread throughout the cosmetic and beauty industry today, but I want to add a word of concern for those who are considering cosmetic surgery. With millions of people watching extreme makeovers on television today, which usually include cosmetic surgeries that are always successful, the appeal and affordability to those in pursuit of beauty has never been higher according to the National Clearinghouse of Plastic Surgery Statistics. When it comes to turning back the aging process, there is no quicker route than cosmetic surgery.

I am often asked by clients for recommendations on cosmetic surgeons, and I have several excellent, certified surgeons whom I recommend. But I always ask the client to push the pause button and make a good evaluation of what will be involved and the possible risks associated with it. I had a dear friend who died from complications of liposuction, which is the most popular cosmetic surgery in America today with over 400,000 of these procedures being done annually. I have also seen numerous cases where the procedures led to disastrous results. Slight variations in technique can result in big problems, depending on the person. Any physician who claims he has never had a problem with his surgeries is either a liar or inexperienced. Every surgery has risks.

Here's what I've discovered about liposuction, which promises to remove fat cells to produce smoother contours. While it should be one of the safest procedures in cosmetic surgery, it has led to a number of death in the U.S. Since its introduction in the early 1970s, liposuction has been refined but remains a brutal process. The technique of tumescent liposuction involves pumping several quarts of a solution below the skin in the area to be suctioned.

The saline solution includes lidocaine, a local anesthetic to numb the surgical site, and epinephrine, a vessel-constrictor to help limit bleeding. The skillful use of the fluid is the most critical factor in the patient's safety. The fat is then suctioned out through tubes.

The problem is that there is often a severe lack of training in these procedures. According to the *Plastic Reconstruction Surgery* journal, nearly half the lipoplasties performed in America during 1996 were not board-certified for plastic surgery. Indeed, anyone with a medical license—from dentists to dermatologists to obstetricians to pediatricians—can take a short course in it and then perform them. In "The Lethal Politics of Beauty" article in the June 2000 edition of *George* magazine, Michael Gross reported, "Most states have no rules that regulate surgery or the administration of anesthesia; set standards for monitoring, staffing, recovery rooms, and operating room personnel, or mandate reporting of deaths or untoward incidents related to anesthesia and surgery.... As things stand now, only California requires surgical offices to be accredited, and surgeons to have hospital privileges." The reality is that the surgery is only as good as the surgeon.

People considering this surgery need to understand the facts and plan for the best and worst possibilities. If one doctor will do a procedure for one-tenth the price of another doctor, consider the source before you say yes. Dr. Gerald Imber, M.D., a plastic surgeon in New York City, says, "You need skill, judgment, experience, and knowledge in a crisis. Idiots try to make a size 14 a size 6, and they run the risk of killing the patient. If you lose too much fluid, your circulatory system can collapse. Or a fat embolism—a piece of fat—can break free, lodge in the lungs, and cause pneumonia." Another significant danger lies in the toxicity of the lidocaine-epinephrine solution and its interactions with other medications the patient may be taking. If the surgeon is not skilled, it is possible to perforate the abdominal wall or internal organs. There are also many situations where the patient is left with sacks of skin where the fat once occupied space.

Dr. Yoho of the Cosmetic Surgery Education Center says, "Cosmetic surgery is often a trade-off between good results and potential for problems. Read this last sentence again. It is a key concept. In other words, your chance for the best possible result may be related to how much surgery you have, and with more surgery, there is more chance of a problem. For example, with a face peel, the chance of scarring and the removal of wrinkles is increased with deeper peeling. The doctor has to judge just where to stop. This is easier with the laser than with the old acid peels or dermabrasion, but variables such as skin thickness and infection may change the result. There's just no way to do any surgery in a perfectly exact way to get perfect results every time without any risk of problems."

That is true across the board—from wrinkle-reducing procedures to face lifts to implants. While we want to only see the positives, there are also serious complications to consider. For instance, although implants may promise a Barbie bosom that turns men's heads on a swivel, you face possible infections, fluid collection, imperfections, and slow healing. Tissue can build up around the implant and start to squeeze it. It is possible for them to tear or rip and deflate. Consider that when your sixteen-year-old daughter wants implants to help her look bigger. Chances for complications may be slender, but they are definite.

Surgery is surgery, even if it's called cosmetic. First, consider your motivation for seeking it. Is it worth the risk? If so, then consider the qualifications of your surgeon. Do not enter into it without absolute confidence in his or her qualifications. It is your life.

CONCLUSION

If beauty is something you keep thinking you can buy through a surgeon, or in a cosmetic product, or through a quick-fix diet, you'll be willing to sacrifice yourself to try to get it. But if beauty is something you feel about yourself . . . about an inner happiness and joy that no one can take away from you, you'll value yourself too much to risk damaging your body through cosmetics with potentially harmful ingredients or through risky surgeries or herbal supplements that promise to burn the fat away. Be wise in your pursuits. You never need to be dying to be beautiful!

> *"Beauty is in the eye of the beholder . . .*
> *but it is also in the eye of the possessor.*
> *What makes us truly attractive to others*
> *is the projection of our self-esteem."*
> —PETER LAMAS

PETER LAMAS is Founder of Lamas Beauty International as well as its principal product developer. Lamas Beauty International is one of the fastest growing and respected natural beauty products manufacturers in the United States. Their award-winning products are regarded as among the cleanest, purest, and most innovative in the beauty industry—products that are a synergy of *Beauty, Nature, and Science*. The company philosophy is to produce products that are safe, effective, free of harmful chemicals, environmentally friendly, and cruelty free. They insure that their products are free of animal ingredients and animal byproducts.

All of the Lamas Beauty International products can been seen and ordered from their web site, www.lamasbeauty.com. To contact them for a complete product catalog and order form or to place an order, please call toll free (888) 738-7621, Fax (713) 869-3266, or write:

LAMAS BEAUTY INTERNATIONAL
5535 Memorial Drive Ste. #F355
Houston, TX 77007

Lamas Beauty offers a full range of hair-care, body-care, and skin-care products. Some of the most recommended products include the following:

Pro-Vita C Vital Infusion Complex: Highly potent anti-aging cream that helps improve premature aging skin. Applied nightly, it defends, nourishes, and stimulates skin through a combination of three powerful antioxidants—*Vitamin C-Ester*, *Alpha Lipoic Acid*, and *DMAE* —all of which fight free radicals and help restore firm, supple, youthful-looking skin. Advanced delivery system encourages the skin's ability to regenerate, increases the skin's firmness and elasticity, minimizes the appearance of fine lines and wrinkles, and helps nurture mature skin.

Pro-Vita C Moisturizer SPF 15: Distinguished as "Best Product of the Year" by *Health Magazine*, as judged by dermatologists across the United States. A potent, multi-action formula to maximize protection during the day. Contains a high percentage of highly absorbable L-Ascorbic Vitamin C (one of nature's most powerful antioxidants), SPF 15 sunscreen protection against ultraviolet rays (UVA, UVB, and UVC rays), Hyaluronic Acid for intensive moisturizing, Vitamins A and E and Retinyl Palmitate (a derivative of wrinkle-smoothing Retin-A) in a unique delivery system.

Chinese Herb Stimulating Shampoo: A therapeutic special-care formula empowered with Chinese herbs used for centuries to promote healthy hair growth, stimulate and energize weak hair and scalp. Gently removes hair follicle-blocking sebum and debris that can slow growth and cause premature hair loss. This formula is mild and gentle and won't irritate, strip away color, or dehydrate hair or scalp. Helps alleviate dandruff and itchiness.

Firming & Brightening Eye Complex: Distinguished as "Product of the Year" by *DaySpa Magazine*. The major benefit of this anti-aging eye cream is its ability to lighten dark shadows and circles under the eyes through the unique natural ingredient, *Emblica*, which is extracted from the *Phyllanthus Emblica fruit* (a medicinal plant used in Ayurvedic medicine). Emblica has been shown to soften age signs, deep wrinkles, and lines as much as 68–90 percent in independent tests. Also provides intensive moisturization through Hyaluronic Acid, one of the most effective and expensive moisturizing ingredients available.

Unleash Your Greatness

AT BRONZE BOW PUBLISHING WE ARE COMMITTED
to helping you achieve your **ultimate potential**
in functional athletic strength, fitness, natural
muscular development, and all-around superb
health and youthfulness.

Our books, videos, newsletters, Web sites, and training seminars will bring you the very latest in scientifically validated information that has been carefully extracted and compiled from leading scientific, medical, health, nutritional, and fitness journals worldwide.

Our goal is to empower you! To arm you with the best possible knowledge in all facets of strength and personal development so that you can make the right choices that are appropriate for *you*.

Now, as always, **the difference between greatness and mediocrity** begins with a choice. It is said that knowledge is power. But that statement is a half truth. Knowledge is power only when it has been tested, proven, and applied to your life. At that point knowledge becomes wisdom, and in wisdom there truly is *power*. The power to help you choose wisely.

So join us as we bring you the finest in health-building information and natural strength-training strategies to help you reach your ultimate potential.

FOR INFORMATION ON ALL OUR EXCITING NEW SPORTS AND FITNESS PRODUCTS, CONTACT:

BRONZE BOW PUBLISHING
2600 East 26th Street
Minneapolis, MN 55406

WEB SITES
www.bronzebowpublishing.com
www.masterlevelfitness.com

612.724.8200   Toll Free **866.724.8200**   FAX **612.724.8995**